D0742941

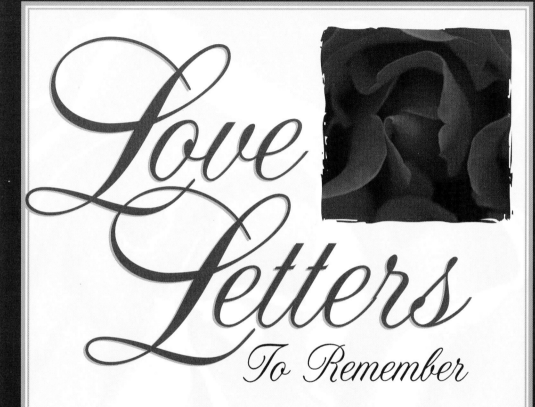

Love Letters
To Remember

AN INTIMATE COLLECTION OF
ROMANCE AND PASSION

ISBN 1-889116-02-5

Printed in the United States of America

First U.S. Edition

Design by Paragon Communications Group, Inc., Tulsa, Oklahoma

Published by
PENBROOKE PUBLISHING
Tulsa, Oklahoma

ACKNOWLEDGMENTS

Byron: *Byron's Letters and Journals,* edited by Leslie Marchand. John Murray Publishers, Ltd. Printed by permission of John Murray Publishers, Ltd.

Duncan, Isadora: Reprinted by permission of The Dance Collection, The New York Public Library for the Performing Arts Astor, Lenox and Tilden Foundations.

Fitzgerald, Zelda: *Zelda, A Biography* by Nancy Milford. Harper and Row Publishers, Inc.

Kafka, Franz: *Letters to Felice* by Franz Kafka, translated by James Stern and Elizabeth Duckworth. English translation copyright © 1973 by Schocken Books, Inc. Reprinted by permission of Schocken Books, published by Pantheon Books, a division of Random House, Inc.

Keats, John: *The Letters of John Keats 1814-1821*, edited by H. E. Rollins. Published by Cambridge University Press in conjunction with Harvard University Press. Reprinted by permission of Cambridge University Press.

Liszt, Franz: *Letters of Franz Liszt*, translated by Constance Bache. H. Grevel and Co., London 1894.

Voltaire: *Voltaire in His Letters,* by S. G. Tallentyre. G. P. Putnam and Sons.

Every effort has been made to locate the copyright owners of the material used in this book. Please let us know if an error has been made, and we will make any necessary changes in subsequent printings.

Love Letters
To Remember

An Intimate Collection of Romance and Passion

PENBROOKE
PUBLISHING

Tulsa, Oklahoma

Presented to:

Grandmother Cook

From:

Sarah Cook

Date:

12 - 25 - 99

Contents

The Love-Letter

Warmed by her hand and shadowed by her hair
As close she leaned and poured her heart through thee,
Whereof the articulate throbs accompany
The smooth black stream that makes thy whiteness fair,—
Sweet fluttering sheet, even of her breath aware,—
Oh let thy silent song disclose to me
That soul wherewith her lips and eyes agree
Like married music in Love's answering air.

Fain had I watched her when, at some fond thought,
Her bosom to the writing closelier press'd,
And her breast's secrets peered into her breast;
When, through eyes raised an instant, her soul sought
My soul, and from the sudden confluence caught
The words that made her love the loveliest.

—Dante Gabriel Rossetti

Zelda Sayre
to
F. Scott Fitzgerald

F. Scott Fitzgerald and Zelda Sayre

It was the Jazz Age and the Fitzgeralds were the trendsetters of their day. Their lavish parties and reckless living became a symbol of New York in the 1920's. The love affair between Francis Scott Key Fitzgerald, famous for such works as *The Great Gatsby* and *This Side of Paradise* and Zelda Sayre, a dancer and later an author herself, was not always a smooth one but it was well known that they had the love of a lifetime.

The couple met at a country club dance in July of 1918. Scott was a first lieutenant in the 67th infantry and just starting out as a writer. He fell in love with Zelda while watching her dance and soon after proposed to her, but she refused. They kept in touch for several months but did not become engaged until Scott signed his first contract with Scribners. The Fitzgeralds were married in April of 1920 and later had a daughter, Scottie, together. The letters that follow were written in the early years of their relationship.

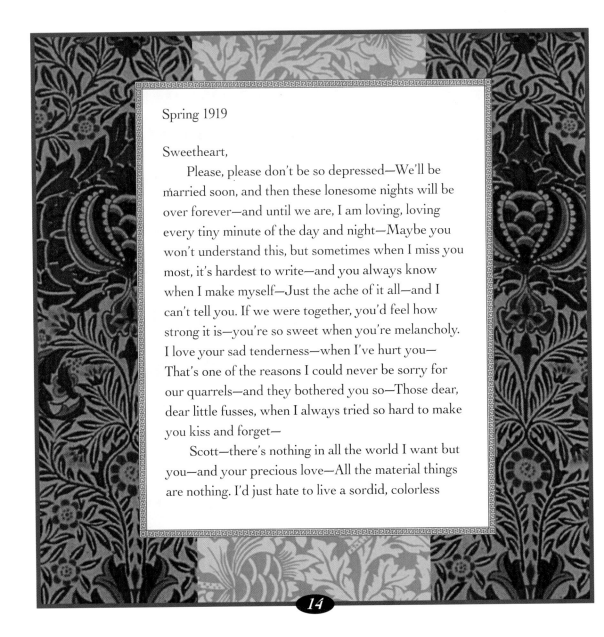

Spring 1919

Sweetheart,

Please, please don't be so depressed—We'll be married soon, and then these lonesome nights will be over forever—and until we are, I am loving, loving every tiny minute of the day and night—Maybe you won't understand this, but sometimes when I miss you most, it's hardest to write—and you always know when I make myself—Just the ache of it all—and I can't tell you. If we were together, you'd feel how strong it is—you're so sweet when you're melancholy. I love your sad tenderness—when I've hurt you— That's one of the reasons I could never be sorry for our quarrels—and they bothered you so—Those dear, dear little fusses, when I always tried so hard to make you kiss and forget—

Scott—there's nothing in all the world I want but you—and your precious love—All the material things are nothing. I'd just hate to live a sordid, colorless existence—because you'd soon love me less—and less—and I'd do anything—anything—to keep your heart for my own—I don't want to live—I want to love first, and live incidentally—Why don't you feel that I'm waiting—I'll come to you, Lover, when you're ready—Don't, don't ever think of the things you can't give me—You've trusted me with the dearest heart of all—and it's so much more than anybody else in all the world has ever had—

How can you think deliberately of life without me—If you should die—O Darling—Darling Scott—It'd be like going blind. I know I would, too,—I'd have no purpose in life—just a pretty—decoration. Don't you think I was made for you? I feel like you had me ordered—and I was delivered to you—to be worn—I want you to wear me, like a watch—charm or a button hole boquet—to the world. And then, when we're alone, I want to help—to know that you can't do anything without me. . . .

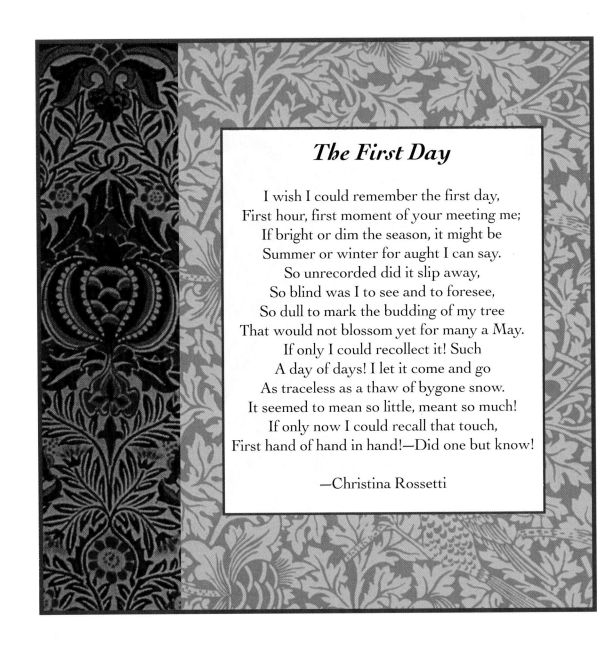

The First Day

I wish I could remember the first day,
First hour, first moment of your meeting me;
If bright or dim the season, it might be
Summer or winter for aught I can say.
So unrecorded did it slip away,
So blind was I to see and to foresee,
So dull to mark the budding of my tree
That would not blossom yet for many a May.
If only I could recollect it! Such
A day of days! I let it come and go
As traceless as a thaw of bygone snow.
It seemed to mean so little, meant so much!
If only now I could recall that touch,
First hand of hand in hand!—Did one but know!

—Christina Rossetti

Napoleon Bonaparte
to
Josephine Beauharnais

Napoleon Bonaparte and Josephine Beauharnais

apoleon Bonaparte, one of the most influential and powerful leaders of the French Revolutionary period is also known for his romantic liaisons. His legendary union with 33-year-old widow Josephine Beauharnais began with a chance meeting. It was Paris, 1795 and Josephine's young son had requested his father's sword as a keepsake. Napoleon, a general at the time, was touched by the request of the patriotic boy and granted it. When Josephine came to thank him, they fell in love. Their early relationship was one of the most passionate ever recorded. Napoleon assumed command of the French Army shortly thereafter and the two were frequently separated. This separation produced a stream of letters from Napoleon filled with passion and yet suspicious of Josephine's whereabouts and dealings. It was this suspicion and other love affairs that brought the marriage to annulment in 1809, only five years after Josephine was crowned Empress. She died alone at their estate in Malmaison in 1814.

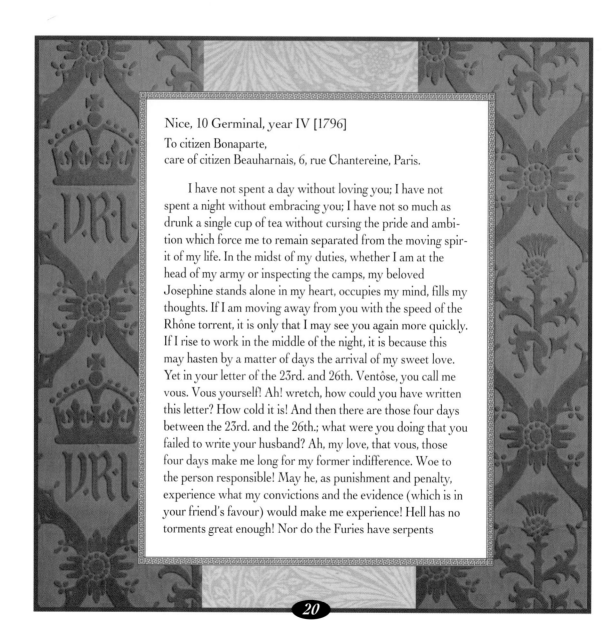

Nice, 10 Germinal, year IV [1796]
To citizen Bonaparte,
care of citizen Beauharnais, 6, rue Chantereine, Paris.

I have not spent a day without loving you; I have not spent a night without embracing you; I have not so much as drunk a single cup of tea without cursing the pride and ambition which force me to remain separated from the moving spirit of my life. In the midst of my duties, whether I am at the head of my army or inspecting the camps, my beloved Josephine stands alone in my heart, occupies my mind, fills my thoughts. If I am moving away from you with the speed of the Rhône torrent, it is only that I may see you again more quickly. If I rise to work in the middle of the night, it is because this may hasten by a matter of days the arrival of my sweet love. Yet in your letter of the 23rd. and 26th. Ventôse, you call me vous. Vous yourself! Ah! wretch, how could you have written this letter? How cold it is! And then there are those four days between the 23rd. and the 26th.; what were you doing that you failed to write your husband? Ah, my love, that vous, those four days make me long for my former indifference. Woe to the person responsible! May he, as punishment and penalty, experience what my convictions and the evidence (which is in your friend's favour) would make me experience! Hell has no torments great enough! Nor do the Furies have serpents

enough! Vous! Vous! Ah! how will things stand in two weeks?
My spirit is heavy; my heart is fettered and I am terrified by my
fantasies. . . .You love me less; but you will get over the loss. One
day you will love me no longer; at least tell me; then I shall know
how I have come to deserve this misfortune . . . .Farewell, my
wife: the torment, joy, hope and moving spirit of my life; whom I
love, whom I fear, who fills me with tender feelings which draw
me close to Nature, and with violent impulses as tumultuous as
thunder. I ask of you neither eternal love, nor fidelity, but simply. . . .truth, unlimited honesty. The day when you say 'I love
you less' will mark the end of my love and the last day of my
life. If my heart were base enough to love without being loved in
return I would tear it to pieces. Josephine! Josephine!

Remember what I have sometimes said to you: Nature has
endowed me with a virile and decisive character. It has built
yours out of lace and gossamer. Have you ceased to love me?
Forgive me, love of my life, my soul is racked by conflicting
forces.

My heart, obsessed by you, is full of fears which prostrate
me with misery. . . .I am distressed not to be calling you by
name. I shall wait for you to write it.

Farewell! Ah! if you love me less you can never have loved
me. In that case I shall truly be pitiable.

Bonaparte

A Red, Red Rose

O My Luve's like a red, red rose,
That's newly sprung in June;
O My Luve's like the melodie
That's sweetly played in tune.

As fair art thou, my bonnie lass,
So deep in luve am I;
And I will luve thee still, my dear,
Till a' the seas gang dry.

Till a' the seas gang dry, my dear,
And the rocks melt wi' the sun:
O I will love thee still, my dear,
While the sands o' life shall run.

And fare thee weel, my only luve,
And fare thee weel awhile!
And I will come again, my luve,
Though it were ten thousand mile.

—Robert Burns

Ludwig van Beethoven
to his
"Immortal Beloved"

Beethoven and his "Immortal Beloved"

udwig van Beethoven (1770-1827), one of history's most famous and mysterious composers died at the age of 57 with one great secret. Upon his death, the following letter was found among his possessions. It was written to an unknown woman who Beethoven simply called his "Immortal Beloved." The world may never put a face with this mysterious woman or know the circumstances of their affair and his letters are all that is left of a love as intensely passionate as the music for which Beethoven became famous. Compositions such as the *Moonlight Sonata* as well as Beethoven's many symphonies express eloquently the tragedy of a relationship never publicly realized.

July 6, [1806]

My angel, my all, my very self—only a few words today and at that with your pencil—not till tomorrow will my lodgings be definitively determined upon—what a useless waste of time. Why this deep sorrow where necessity speaks—can our love endure except through sacrifices—except through not demanding everything—can you change it that you are not wholly mine, I not wholly thine?

Oh, God! look out into the beauties of nature and comfort yourself with that which must be—love demands everything and that very justly—thus it is with me so far as you are concerned, and you with me. If we were wholly united you would feel the pain of it as little as I!

My journey was a fearful one; I did not reach here until 4 o'clock yesterday morning; lacking horses the post coach chose another route—but what an awful one.

At the stage before the last I was warned not to travel at night—made fearful of a forest, but that only made me the more eager and I was wrong; the coach must need break down on the wretched road, a

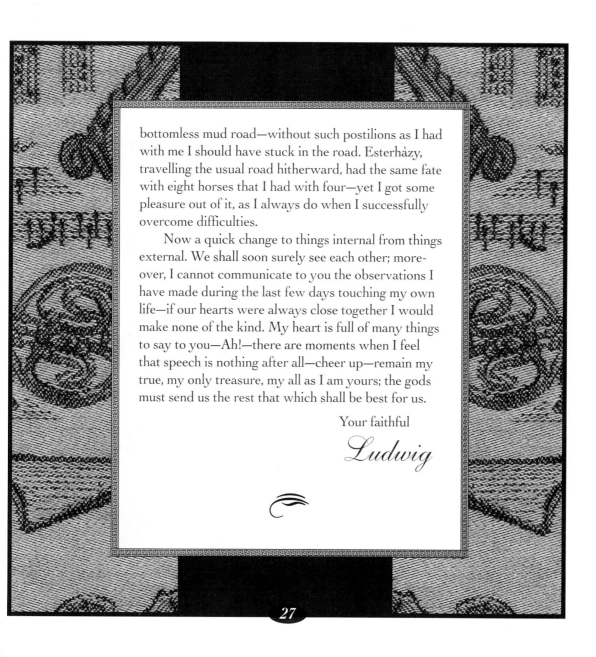

bottomless mud road—without such postilions as I had with me I should have stuck in the road. Esterhàzy, travelling the usual road hitherward, had the same fate with eight horses that I had with four—yet I got some pleasure out of it, as I always do when I successfully overcome difficulties.

Now a quick change to things internal from things external. We shall soon surely see each other; moreover, I cannot communicate to you the observations I have made during the last few days touching my own life—if our hearts were always close together I would make none of the kind. My heart is full of many things to say to you—Ah!—there are moments when I feel that speech is nothing after all—cheer up—remain my true, my only treasure, my all as I am yours; the gods must send us the rest that which shall be best for us.

Your faithful

Ludwig

How Do I Love Thee?
Let Me Count the Ways

How do I love thee? Let me count the ways.
I love thee to the depth and breadth and height
My soul can reach, when feeling out of sight
For the ends of Being and ideal Grace.
I love thee to the level of every day's
Most quiet need, by sun and candlelight.
I love thee freely, as men strive for Right;
I love thee purely, as they turn from Praise.
I love thee with the passion put to use
In my old griefs, and with my childhood's faith.
I love thee with a love I seemed to lose
With my lost saints,—I love thee with the breath,
Smiles, tears, of all my life!—and, if God choose,
I shall love thee better after death.

—Elizabeth Barrett Browning

Voltaire
to
Olympe Dunover

Francios-Marie Arouet (Voltaire) and Olympe Dunover

Voltaire (1694-1778), French author and philosopher, wrote this passionate letter to his mistress while in prison. At the age of nineteen Voltaire was sent as an attaché to the French Ambassador to the Netherlands. It was there that he fell in love with Olympe Dunover, the poor daughter of a lower-class woman. Their affair was not approved of by either the ambassador or Olympe's mother and Voltaire was soon imprisoned to keep them apart.

Shortly after, Voltaire managed to escape by climbing out of the window. He flew to his lover and they made plans to escape to Paris. However, these plans never came to pass. The two were intercepted, Voltaire was sent back to Paris and Olympe eventually married the Count of Winterfield, yet she and Voltaire remained intimate until her death in 1749.

The Hague, 1713.

I am a prisoner here in the name of the King; they can take my life, but not the love that I feel for you. Yes, my adorable mistress, to-night I shall see you, and if I had to put my head on the block to do it. For Heaven's sake, do not speak to me in such disastrous terms as you write; you must live and be cautious; beware of madame your mother as of your worst enemy. What do I say? Beware of everybody, trust no one; keep yourself in readiness, as soon as the moon is visible; I shall leave the hotel incognito, take a carriage or a chaise, we shall drive like the wind to Sheveningen; I shall take paper and ink with me; we shall write our letters. If you love me, reassure your-self, and call all your strength and presence of mind to your aid; do not let your mother notice anything, try to have your picture, and be assured that the menace of the greatest tortures will not prevent me to serve you. No, nothing has the power to part me from you; our love is based upon virtue, and will last as long as our lives. Adieu, there is nothing that I will not brave for your sake; you deserve much more than that. Adieu, my dear heart!

Arouet
(Voltaire)

*The course of true love never
did run smooth.
—William Shakespeare*

The Bargain

My true love hath my heart, and I have his,
By just exchange one for another given;
I hold his dear, and mine he cannot miss,
There never was a better bargain driven:
My true love hath my heart, and I have his.

His heart in me keeps him and me in one,
My heart in him his thoughts and senses guides;
He loves my heart, for once it was his own,
I cherish his because in me it bides:
My true love hath my heart, and I have his.

—Sir Philip Sidney

Lord Byron
to
Countess Teresa Guiccioli

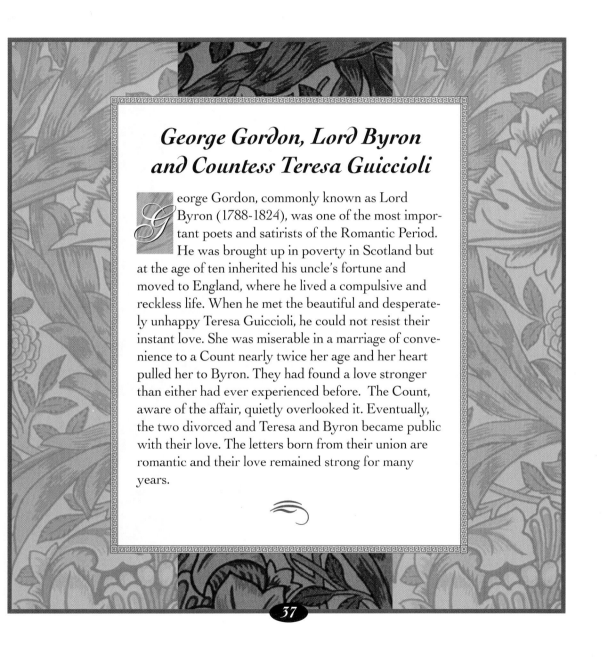

George Gordon, Lord Byron and Countess Teresa Guiccioli

eorge Gordon, commonly known as Lord Byron (1788-1824), was one of the most important poets and satirists of the Romantic Period. He was brought up in poverty in Scotland but at the age of ten inherited his uncle's fortune and moved to England, where he lived a compulsive and reckless life. When he met the beautiful and desperately unhappy Teresa Guiccioli, he could not resist their instant love. She was miserable in a marriage of convenience to a Count nearly twice her age and her heart pulled her to Byron. They had found a love stronger than either had ever experienced before. The Count, aware of the affair, quietly overlooked it. Eventually, the two divorced and Teresa and Byron became public with their love. The letters born from their union are romantic and their love remained strong for many years.

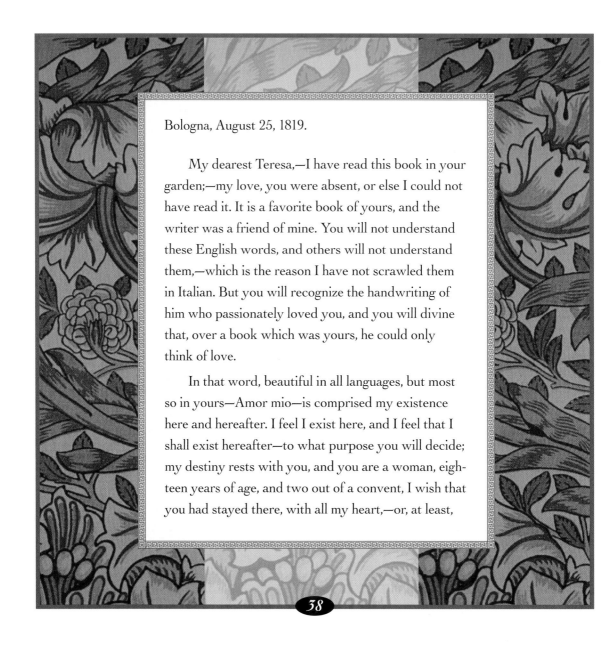

Bologna, August 25, 1819.

My dearest Teresa,—I have read this book in your garden;—my love, you were absent, or else I could not have read it. It is a favorite book of yours, and the writer was a friend of mine. You will not understand these English words, and others will not understand them,—which is the reason I have not scrawled them in Italian. But you will recognize the handwriting of him who passionately loved you, and you will divine that, over a book which was yours, he could only think of love.

In that word, beautiful in all languages, but most so in yours—Amor mio—is comprised my existence here and hereafter. I feel I exist here, and I feel that I shall exist hereafter—to what purpose you will decide; my destiny rests with you, and you are a woman, eighteen years of age, and two out of a convent, I wish that you had stayed there, with all my heart,—or, at least, that I had never met you in your married state.

But all this is too late. I love you, and you love me,—at least, you say so, and act as if you did so, which last is a great consolation in all events. But I more than love you, and cannot cease to love you.

Think of me, sometimes, when the Alps and ocean divide us,—but they never will, unless you wish it.

Byron

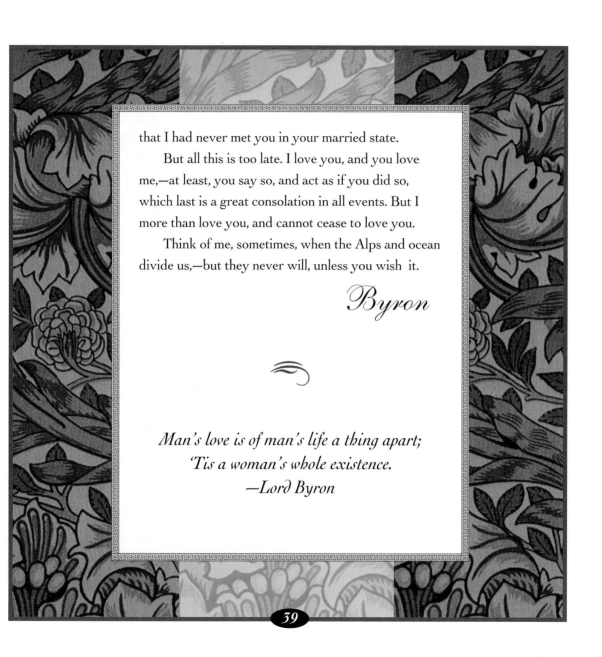

Man's love is of man's life a thing apart;
'Tis a woman's whole existence.
—Lord Byron

She Walks in Beauty, Like the Night

She walks in beauty, like the night
Of cloudless climes and starry skies;
And all that's best of dark and bright
Meet in her aspect and her eyes;
Thus mellowed to that tender light
Which heaven to gaudy day denies.

One shade the more, one ray the less,
Had half impaired the nameless grace
Which waves in every raven tress
Or softly lightens o'er her face;
Where thoughts serenely sweet express
How pure, how dear their dwelling place.

And on that cheek, and o'er that brow
So soft, so calm, yet eloquent,
The smiles that win, the tints that glow,
But tell of days in goodness spent,
A mind at peace with all below,
A heart whose love is innocent!

—George Gordon, Lord Byron

Robert Schumann
to
Clara Schumann

Robert and Clara Schumann

Robert Schumann, the seventeenth century German composer and pianist is known for such enduring achievements as the opera *Genoveva* and piano pieces, *Carnaval* and *Fantasiestucke*. He first fell in love with Clara Wieck during his early piano training under the instruction of her father, Friederich Wieck. Clara herself was a virtuoso pianist and her father was bitterly opposed to the match. Persistent to marry her, Robert went to court to seek legal consent. His love eventually won out and the couple was soon married.

Robert and Clara led a frantic but rewarding life. To a large extent their lives revolved around their musical interests. However, the couple managed to have eight children together. Throughout their many years of marriage, countless love letters were exchanged between Robert and Clara, even in the midst of extreme difficulties with health and career. Through these letters it is apparent to the world that they shared a lifetime of tender devotion.

1838
The 2nd

How happy your last letters have made me—those since Christmas Eve! I should like to call you by all the endearing epithets, and yet I can find no lovelier word than the simple word 'dear,' but there is a particular way of saying it. My dear one, then, I have wept for joy to think that you are mine, and often wonder if I deserve you. One would think that no one man's heart and brain could stand all the things that are crowded into one day. Where do these thousands of thoughts, wishes, sorrows, joys and hopes come from? Day in, day out, the procession goes on. But how light-hearted I was yesterday and the day before! There shone out of your letters so noble a spirit, such faith, such a wealth of love! What would I not do for love of you, my own Clara! The knights of old were better off; they could go through fire or slay dragons to win their ladies, but we of today have to content ourselves with more prosaic methods, such as smoking fewer cigars, and the like. After all, though, we can love, knights or no knights; and so, as ever, only the times change, not men's hearts. . . .

You cannot think how your letter has raised and

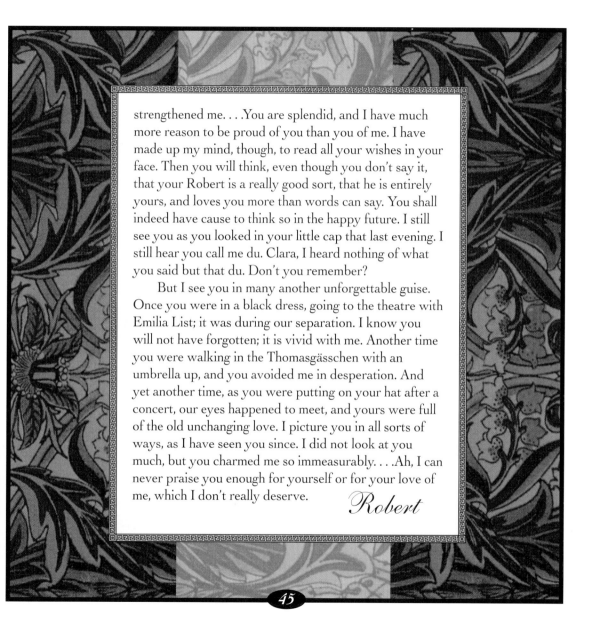

strengthened me. . . .You are splendid, and I have much more reason to be proud of you than you of me. I have made up my mind, though, to read all your wishes in your face. Then you will think, even though you don't say it, that your Robert is a really good sort, that he is entirely yours, and loves you more than words can say. You shall indeed have cause to think so in the happy future. I still see you as you looked in your little cap that last evening. I still hear you call me du. Clara, I heard nothing of what you said but that du. Don't you remember?

But I see you in many another unforgettable guise. Once you were in a black dress, going to the theatre with Emilia List; it was during our separation. I know you will not have forgotten; it is vivid with me. Another time you were walking in the Thomasgässchen with an umbrella up, and you avoided me in desperation. And yet another time, as you were putting on your hat after a concert, our eyes happened to meet, and yours were full of the old unchanging love. I picture you in all sorts of ways, as I have seen you since. I did not look at you much, but you charmed me so immeasurably. . . .Ah, I can never praise you enough for yourself or for your love of me, which I don't really deserve.

Robert

To My Dear and Loving Husband

If ever two were one, then surely we.
If ever man were loved by wife, then thee;
If ever wife was happy in a man,
Compare with me, ye women, if you can.
I prize thy love more than whole mines of gold,
Or all the riches that the East doth hold.
My love is such that rivers cannot quench,
Nor aught but love from thee give recompense.
Thy love is such I can no way repay;
The heavens reward thee manifold, I pray.
Then while we live, in love let's so persevere,
That when we live no more we may live ever.

—Anne Bradstreet

Sir Walter Raleigh
to
Elizabeth Raleigh

Sir Walter and
Elizabeth Raleigh

*S*ir Walter Raleigh (1552-1618), English colonizer, courtier, historian and explorer, was an early advocate of establishing English settlements in newly discovered North America. A favorite courtier of Queen Elizabeth II, he was knighted by her in 1584. His life was one of great accomplishment and triumph, ending tragically with execution.

In 1603 Raleigh was wrongly tried and convicted of treason against the crown, having been set up by one of his enemies in the royal court. His sentence was immediate death. Imprisoned in the Tower of London on what he believed was the eve of his execution, he composed this loving farewell to his wife, Elizabeth.

He was not executed the following morning but remained confined in the Tower of London until 1616, when he was released to lead an expedition in search of gold for the crown. However, this did not mark his freedom and in 1618 he was returned to the Tower of London and executed at the harsh hand of Queen Elizabeth II's successor, James I.

[1603]

You shall now receive (my dear wife) my last words in these my last lines. My love I send you that you may keep it when I am dead, and my counsel that you may remember it when I am no more. I would not by my will present you with sorrows (dear Besse) let them go to the grave with me and be buried in the dust. And seeing that it is not God's will that I should see you any more in this life, bear it patiently, and with a heart like thy self.

First, I send you all the thanks which my heart can conceive, or my words can rehearse for your many travails, and care taken for me, which though they have not taken effect as you wished, yet my debt to you is not the less: but pay it I never shall in this world.

Secondly, I beseech you for the love you bear me living, do not hide your self many days, but by your travails seek to help your miserable fortunes and the right of your poor child. Thy mourning cannot avail me, I am but dust. . . .

Remember your poor child for his father's sake,

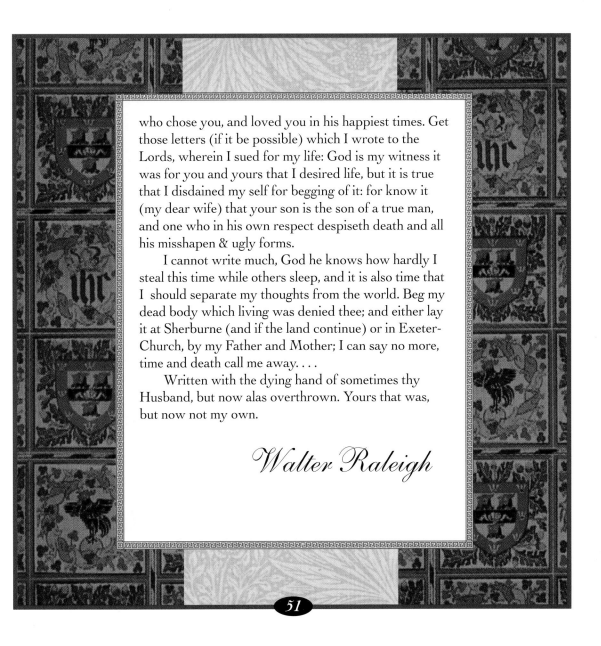

who chose you, and loved you in his happiest times. Get those letters (if it be possible) which I wrote to the Lords, wherein I sued for my life: God is my witness it was for you and yours that I desired life, but it is true that I disdained my self for begging of it: for know it (my dear wife) that your son is the son of a true man, and one who in his own respect despiseth death and all his misshapen & ugly forms.

I cannot write much, God he knows how hardly I steal this time while others sleep, and it is also time that I should separate my thoughts from the world. Beg my dead body which living was denied thee; and either lay it at Sherburne (and if the land continue) or in Exeter-Church, by my Father and Mother; I can say no more, time and death call me away. . . .

Written with the dying hand of sometimes thy Husband, but now alas overthrown. Yours that was, but now not my own.

Walter Raleigh

Now What Is Love?

Now what is Love, I pray thee, tell?
It is that fountain and that well
Where pleasure and repentance dwell;
It is, perhaps the sauncing bell
That tolls all into heaven or hell;
And this is Love, as I hear tell.

Yet what is Love, I prithee, say?
It is a work on holiday,
It is December matched with May,
When lusty bloods in fresh array
Hear ten months after the play;
And this is Love, as I hear say.

Yet what is Love, good shepherd, sain?
It is a yes, it is a nay,
A pretty kind of sporting fray,
It is thing will soon away.
Then, nymphs, take vantage while ye may;
And this is Love, as I hear say.

Yet what is Love, good shepherd, show?
A thing that creeps, it cannot go,
A prize that passeth to and fro,
A thing for one, a thing for moe,
And he that proves shall find it so;
And shepherd, this is Love, I trow.

—Walter Raleigh

Count Gabriel Honore
de Mirbeau
to
Sophie de Monnier

Count Gabriel Honore de Mirbeau and Sophie de Monnier

O f all the famous French Revolutionary figures, none is more scandalous than the boisterous Count Gabriel Honore de Mirbeau, author of such shocking literary works as *The Prussian Monarchy Under Frederick the Great* and *The Secret History of the Count of Berlin.*

However, his reputation was not simply that of a writer but that of a womanizer as well. His gruff exterior and enormous size should have been repulsive to women but indeed it wasn't. Women were attracted to him in droves. His history includes a long succession of seductions and torrid affairs, including a liaison with the Marquis of Monnier, Sophie de Monnier. The two were united just long enough to produce a string of letters, such as this one, filled with passion.

c. 1780

To be with the people one loves, says La Bruyère
is enough—to dream you are speaking to them, not
speaking to them, thinking of them, thinking of the
most indifferent things, but by their side, nothing else
matters. O *mon amie*, how true that is! and it is also
true that when one acquires such a habit, it becomes a
necessary part of one's existence. Alas! I well know, I
should know too well, since the three months that I
sigh, far away from thee, that I possess thee no more,
that my happiness has departed. However, when
every morning I wake up, I look for you, it seems to
me that half of myself is missing, and that is too true.
Twenty times during the day, I ask myself where you
are; judge how strong the illusion is, and how cruel it
is to see it vanish. When I go to bed, I do not fail to
make room for you; I push myself quite close to the
wall and leave a great empty space in my small bed.
This movement is mechanical, these thoughts are

involuntary. Ah! how one accustoms oneself to happiness. Alas! one only knows it well when one has lost it, and I'm sure we have only learnt to appreciate how necessary we are to each other, since the thunderbolt has parted us. The source of our tears has not dried up, dear Sophie; we cannot become healed; we have enough in our hearts to love always, and, because of that, enough to weep always. Let those prate who affirm that they have shaken off a great affliction by virtue or by strength of mind; they only became consoled because they are weak and on the surface. There are losses one must never be reconciled to; and when one can no longer bring happiness to what one loves, then one must bring misfortune. Let us speak the Truth itself, it must be; and this delicate sentiment, whatever one may say, is in the nature of a tender love. Would Sophie not be in despair, if she knew her Gabriel consoled?

Love's Philosophy

The fountains mingle with the river
And the rivers with the Ocean,
The winds of Heaven mix for ever
With a sweet emotion;
Nothing in the world is single;
All things by a law divine
In one spirit meet and mingle.
Why not I with thine?—

See the mountains kiss high Heaven
And the waves clasp one another;
No sister-flower would be forgiven
If it disdained its brother;
And the sunlight clasps the earth
And the moonbeams kiss the sea:
What is all this sweet work worth
If thou kiss not me?

—Percy Bysshe Shelley

John Keats
to
Fanny Brawne

John Keats and Fanny Brawne

he story of John Keats and Fanny Brawne is one of literary tragedy. Keats, a leading poet of the nineteenth century, produced such influential works as *Ode on a Grecian Urn* and the epic poem, *Hyperion* during his short life. He was also the author of countless letters to family and friends, his most famous being the letters to Fanny Brawne.

Keats met Fanny in November of 1818 and fell instantly in love with her, to the dismay of both her family and his contemporaries. The couple became secretly engaged soon after. However, fate was working against them. In the winter of 1820, Keats became very ill. He was diagnosed with tuberculosis. The lovers were separated and corresponded only through letters and gifts.

Keats' health progressively declined and in a final effort to save his own life, he moved to Italy. His hope that the dry climate and warmer weather would make him better came to nothing and in 1821, at the age of 25, he was laid to rest. Buried with him, close to his heart, was an unopened letter from Fanny.

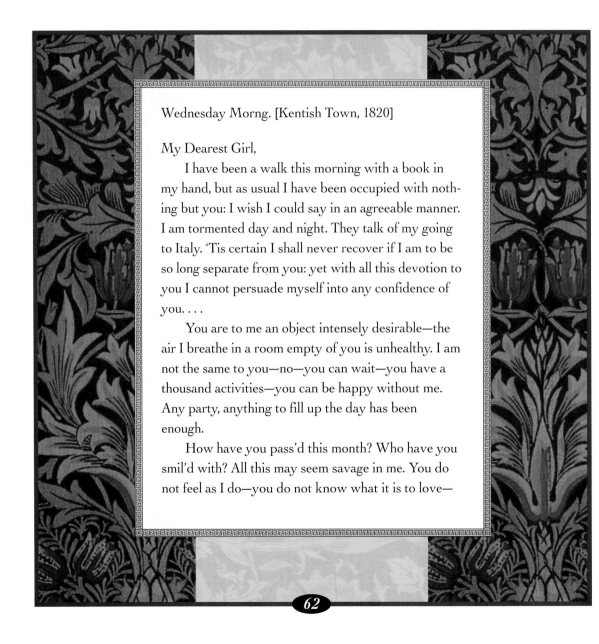

Wednesday Morng. [Kentish Town, 1820]

My Dearest Girl,

I have been a walk this morning with a book in
my hand, but as usual I have been occupied with nothing but you: I wish I could say in an agreeable manner.
I am tormented day and night. They talk of my going
to Italy. 'Tis certain I shall never recover if I am to be
so long separate from you: yet with all this devotion to
you I cannot persuade myself into any confidence of
you. . . .

You are to me an object intensely desirable—the
air I breathe in a room empty of you is unhealthy. I am
not the same to you—no—you can wait—you have a
thousand activities—you can be happy without me.
Any party, anything to fill up the day has been
enough.

How have you pass'd this month? Who have you
smil'd with? All this may seem savage in me. You do
not feel as I do—you do not know what it is to love—

one day you may—your time is not come. . . .

I cannot live without you, and not only you but chaste you; virtuous you. The Sun rises and sets, the day passes, and you follow the bent of your inclination to a certain extent—you have no conception of the quantity of miserable feeling that passes through me in a day—Be serious! Love is not a plaything—and again do not write unless you can do it with a crystal conscience. I would sooner die for want of you than——

Yours for ever

J. Keats

Even when I am not thinking of you I receive your influence and a tenderer nature stealing upon me. All my thoughts, my unhappiest days and nights, have I find not at all cured me of my love of Beauty, but made it so intense that I am miserable when you are not with me.

—John Keats to Fanny Brawne, 1819

Romeo and Juliet

ROMEO
It is my lady, O, it is my love.
O, that she knew she were!
She speaks, yet she says nothing. What of that?
I am too bold. 'Tis not to me she speaks.
Two of the fairest stars in all the heaven,
Having some business, do entreat her eyes
To twinkle in their spheres till they return.
What if her eyes were there, they in her head?
The brightness of her cheek would shame those stars
As daylight doth a lamp; her eyes in heaven
Would through the airy region stream so bright
That birds would sing and think it were not night.
See how she leans her cheek upon her hand!
O, that I were a glove upon that hand,
That I might touch that cheek! . . .

JULIET
O Romeo, Romeo, wherefore art thou Romeo?
Deny thy father and refuse thy name!
Or, if thou wilt not, be but sworn my love,
And I'll no longer be a Capulet. . . .

—William Shakespeare

Heloise
to
Abelard

Heloise and Abelard

The story of Heloise and Abelard is one of tragic love. Abelard, a famous cleric in medieval France met Heloise, a beautiful girl of 16 who had just completed her studies at a convent school and was living with her uncle. Abelard arranged to move into their home and in exchange, he offered to continue Heloise's education. Heloise and Abelard soon fell in love. Aware of her uncle's disapproval, they kept their love a secret. When the uncle did find out, he threw Abelard out. The lovers corresponded secretly for Heloise had discovered she was pregnant. Abelard stole her away to his sister's house in the country where she gave birth to a son. The lovers soon married; her enraged uncle consented, silently vowing his revenge. In order to spare Heloise, Abelard sent her back to the convent where she had been educated. Soon after, her uncle hired thugs to beat and castrate Abelard. Unable to stand this humiliation, he renounced his marriage vows and became a Benedictine monk, just a few miles away from the convent where Heloise was staying. Unable to bear her grief, Heloise became a nun and remained at the convent. The lovers were never together again. Instead, their love was expressed in countless letters sent to each other until Abelard's death at the age of 62. Upon her death, Heloise was buried next to him.

Heloise to Abelard

My tears, which I could not restrain, have blotted half your letter; I wish they had effaced the whole, and that I had returned it to you in that condition; I should then have been satisfied with the little time I kept it; but it was demanded of me too soon.

I must confess I was much easier in my mind before I read your letter. Surely all the misfortunes of lovers are conveyed to them through the eyes: upon reading your letter I feel all mine renewed. I reproached myself for having been so long without venting my sorrows, when the rage of our unrelenting enemies still burns with the same fury. . . .

Let me have faithful account of all that concerns you; I would know everything, be it ever so unfortunate. Perhaps by mingling my sighs with yours I may make your sufferings less, for it is said that all sorrows divided are made lighter. . . .

I have your picture in my room; I never pass it without stopping to look at it; and yet when you are present with me I scarce ever cast my eyes on it. If a picture, which is but a mute representation of an object, can give such pleasure, what cannot letters inspire? They have souls; they can speak; they have in them all that force which expresses the transports of the heart; they have all the fire of our passions, they can raise them as much as if the persons themselves were present; they have all the tenderness and the delicacy of speech, and sometimes even a boldness of expression beyond it.

We may write to each other; so innocent a pleasure is not denied us. Let us not lose through negligence the only happiness which is left us, and the only one perhaps which the malice of our enemies can never ravish from us. I shall read that you are my husband and you shall see me sign myself your wife. In spite of all our misfortunes you may be what you please in your letter. Letters were first invented for consoling such solitary wretches as myself. Having lost the substantial pleasures of seeing and possessing you, I shall in some measure compensate this loss by the satisfaction I shall find in your writing. There I shall read your most sacred thoughts; I shall carry them always about with me, I shall kiss them every moment; if you can be capable of any jealousy let it be for the fond caresses I shall bestow upon your letters, and envy only the happiness of those rivals. . . .

A Farewell

With all my will, but much against my heart,
We two now part.
My Very Dear,
Our solace is, the sad road lies so clear.
It needs no art,
With faint, averted feet
And many a tear,
In our opposed paths to persevere.
Go thou to East, I West.
We will not say
There's any hope, it is so far away
But, O, my Best,
When the one darling of our widowhead,
The nursling Grief, Is dead,
And no dews blur our eyes
To see the peach-bloom come in evening skies,
Perchance we may,
Where now this night is day,
And even through faith of still averted feet,
Making full circle of our banishment,
Amazed meet:
The bitter journey to the bourne so sweet
Seasoning the termless feast of our content
With tears of recognition never dry.

—Coventry Patmore

Isadora Duncan
to
Gordon Craig

Isadora Duncan and Gordon Craig

*I*sadora Duncan (1878-1927) was the toast of Europe at the turn of the twentieth century, dancing her way into the hearts of her admirers. The American-born creator of modern dance drew crowds of notable fans to her revolutionary dance performances. It was at one of these performances in Berlin in 1905 that Gordon Craig, a brilliant theater designer and son of renowned actress Ellen Terry, first saw Isadora in person. Gordon admits in his memoirs that he felt speechless, utterly awed. He writes that her movements on the dance floor were both primal and ethereal. At the end of the performance, he met her in her dressing room. On that very evening, while dancing, Isadora claimed she "felt a presence" out in the audience. As a rule, she never looked out but that evening she was drawn to Gordon Craig and upon meeting him, promptly invited him to dinner.

Isadora's beauty and grace touched many hearts during her lifetime but it was Gordon Craig who was for years the recipient of her simple, unembellished love. She had a charming and witty personality that can be seen in this next letter—just one example of many letters written to Gordon Craig.

Christmas Day 1904

Grand Hotel D'Europe
St. Petersbourg
Rue Michel

Just arrived this morning—
Christmas morning
Here its the 12 of December

My Darling—
I don't like it at all. All the Chairs are staring at me
in the most frightful way—And there is a Lady on the
Mantel piece who has taken a Great objection to me—&
I'm awfully scared—
This is no place for a person with a nice cheerful
disposition like me—it looks like those parlors in the
Novels where they plot things—
All night long the train has not been flying over but
going pim de pim over Great fields of snow—vast plains
of snow—Great bare Countries covered with snow
(Walt [Whitman] could have written 'em up fine) and
over all this the Moon shining—& across the window
always a Golden shower of sparks—from the locomo-
tive—it was quite worth seeing and I lay there looking

out on it all & thinking of you—of you, you dearest sweetest best darling—

The City is covered in snow & little sleighs rushing madly about—All things go in sliders of course. I sent you many little missives along the way—Hope they arrived!—

I must go now & wash the soot off & have my Breakfast.

I say this is a fine way to spend one's Christmas—They brought me first into the Great Bridal Suite here but I stoutly refused to stay in it—These rooms are hung in Dark, Dark Green. It would be an awfully good sort of place to indulge any disposition to suicide lingering in an odd corner of one's disposition.

Give my love to Dear Dear No. 11—and to that nice musty little dear Home No. 6 and for your dear self my heart is overflowing with just the most unoriginal old fashiondest sort of love.

Write to me—
& tell me—
I go now to splash

Your

Isadora

A Thunderstorm in Town
(A Reminiscence: 1893)

She wore a new 'terra-cotta' dress,
And we stayed, because of the pelting
storm,
Within the hansom's dry recess,
Though the horse had stopped, yea,
motionless
We sat on, snug and warm.

Then the downpour ceased,
to my sharp sad pain,
And the glass that had screened our
forms before
Flew up, and out she sprang to her door:
I should have kissed her if the rain
Had lasted a minute more.

—Thomas Hardy

Franz Liszt
to the
Countess Marie D'Agoult

Franz Liszt and Marie D'Agoult

Franz Liszt (1811-1886), pianist and composer of the 19th century, took Paris society by storm with his virtuoso performances. Works such as the *Piano Sonata in B* and the *Dante Symphony* made him one of the most influential composers of his era. It was during these years in Paris that Liszt met the young and beautiful Countess D'Agoult. She was unhappily married and in the process of a separation. She fell madly in love with Liszt.

The love affair between Liszt and Marie lasted for ten years. Together they had a son and two daughters. Their relationship produced an exchange of letters that were full of love, encouragement and sometimes rebuke. The following letter was written in 1834, shortly after the couple had begun living together. It was one of many letters written in a similar passionate style.

However, their love was not enough to keep them together. In 1839, painfully unsure of his fidelity to her, Marie left Liszt to begin a new life elsewhere. She later became known as a writer, writing under the pen name of Daniel Stern. Liszt went on to other relationships and died at the age of 74 in Bavaria.

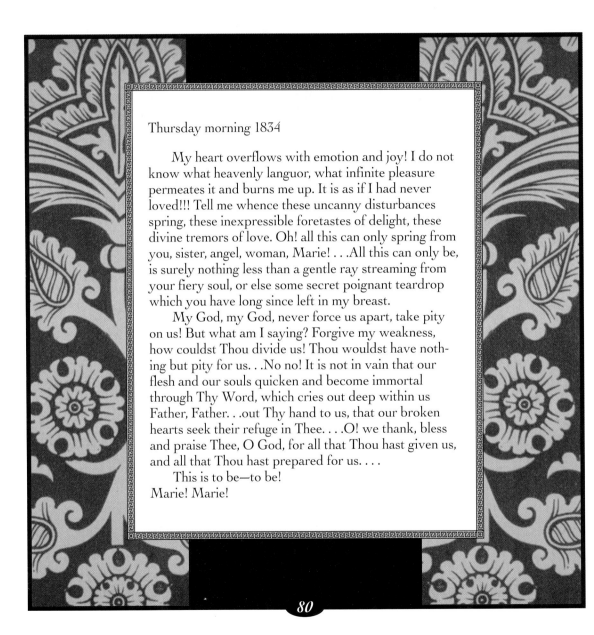

Thursday morning 1834

My heart overflows with emotion and joy! I do not know what heavenly languor, what infinite pleasure permeates it and burns me up. It is as if I had never loved!!! Tell me whence these uncanny disturbances spring, these inexpressible foretastes of delight, these divine tremors of love. Oh! all this can only spring from you, sister, angel, woman, Marie! . . .All this can only be, is surely nothing less than a gentle ray streaming from your fiery soul, or else some secret poignant teardrop which you have long since left in my breast.

My God, my God, never force us apart, take pity on us! But what am I saying? Forgive my weakness, how couldst Thou divide us! Thou wouldst have nothing but pity for us. . .No no! It is not in vain that our flesh and our souls quicken and become immortal through Thy Word, which cries out deep within us Father, Father. . .out Thy hand to us, that our broken hearts seek their refuge in Thee. . . .O! we thank, bless and praise Thee, O God, for all that Thou hast given us, and all that Thou hast prepared for us. . . .

This is to be—to be!
Marie! Marie!

Oh let me repeat that name a hundred times, a thousand times over; for three days now it has lived within me, oppressed me, set me afire. I am not writing to you, no, I am close beside you. I see you, I hear you. Eternity in your arms. . .Heaven, Hell, everything, all is within you, redoubled. . .Oh! Leave me free to rave in my delirium. Drab, tame, constricting reality is no longer enough for me. We must live our lives to the full, loving and suffering to extremes! . . .Oh! you believe me capable of self-sacrifice, chastity, temperance and piety, do you not? But let no more be said of this. . .it is up to you to question, to draw conclusions, to save me as you see fit. Leave me free to rave in my delirium, since you can do nothing, nothing at all for me. This to be! to be!!!

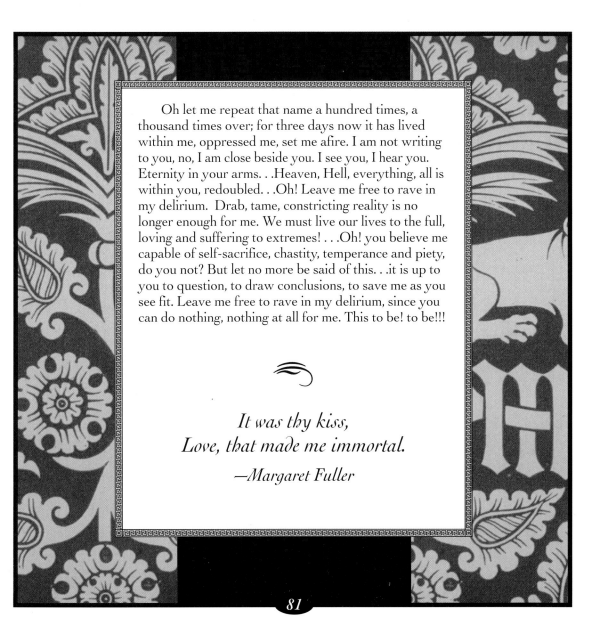

It was thy kiss,
Love, that made me immortal.
—Margaret Fuller

Romance

Romance, who loves to nod and sing,
With drowsy head and folded wing,
Among the green leaves as they shake
Far down within some shadowy lake,
To me a painted paroquet
Hath been—a most familiar bird—
Taught me my alphabet to say—
To lisp my very earliest word
While in the wild wood I did lie,
A child—with a most knowing eye.

Of late, eternal Condor years
So shake the vert Heaven on high
With tumult as they thunder by,
I have no time for idle cares
Through gazing on the unquiet sky.
And when an hour with calmer wings

Its down upon my spirit flings
That little time with lyre and rhyme
To while away—forbidden things!
My heart would feel to be a crime
Unless it trembled with the strings.

—Edgar Allan Poe

Victor Hugo
to
Adèle Foucher

83

Victor Hugo and Adèle Foucher

he French Revolution was made poignantly memorable by the literary works of Victor Hugo (1802-1885). Such works as *Les Miserables* and *The Hunchback of Notre Dame* forever memorialized the plight of the unfortunate working class. Adèle Foucher was Hugo's cousin. They grew up together and at the age of 17, Hugo fell madly in love with her. Adèle was both charming and beautiful and was in love with him as well.

Although both families were opposed to their union, the couple became secretly engaged, determined to marry. For three years they exchanged secret messages. The following letter was written shortly after Hugo was promised a pension from Louis XVIII as a reward for his loyalty. This pension allowed the couple to marry. Their marriage lasted until Adèle's death in 1868.

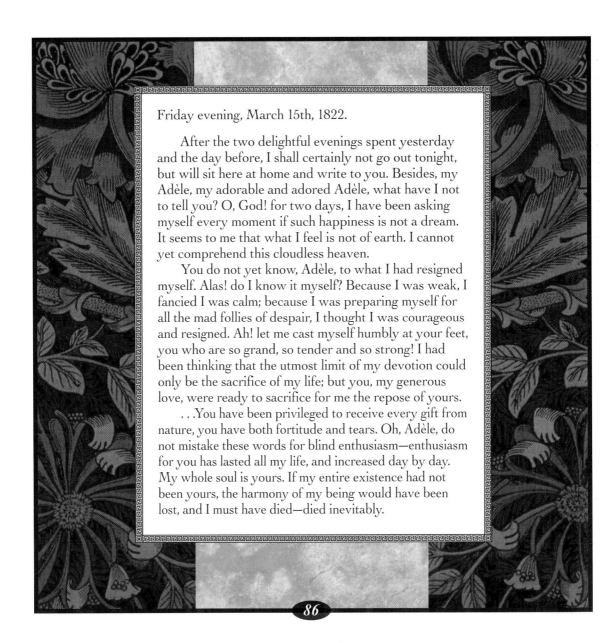

Friday evening, March 15th, 1822.

After the two delightful evenings spent yesterday and the day before, I shall certainly not go out tonight, but will sit here at home and write to you. Besides, my Adèle, my adorable and adored Adèle, what have I not to tell you? O, God! for two days, I have been asking myself every moment if such happiness is not a dream. It seems to me that what I feel is not of earth. I cannot yet comprehend this cloudless heaven.

You do not yet know, Adèle, to what I had resigned myself. Alas! do I know it myself? Because I was weak, I fancied I was calm; because I was preparing myself for all the mad follies of despair, I thought I was courageous and resigned. Ah! let me cast myself humbly at your feet, you who are so grand, so tender and so strong! I had been thinking that the utmost limit of my devotion could only be the sacrifice of my life; but you, my generous love, were ready to sacrifice for me the repose of yours.

. . .You have been privileged to receive every gift from nature, you have both fortitude and tears. Oh, Adèle, do not mistake these words for blind enthusiasm—enthusiasm for you has lasted all my life, and increased day by day. My whole soul is yours. If my entire existence had not been yours, the harmony of my being would have been lost, and I must have died—died inevitably.

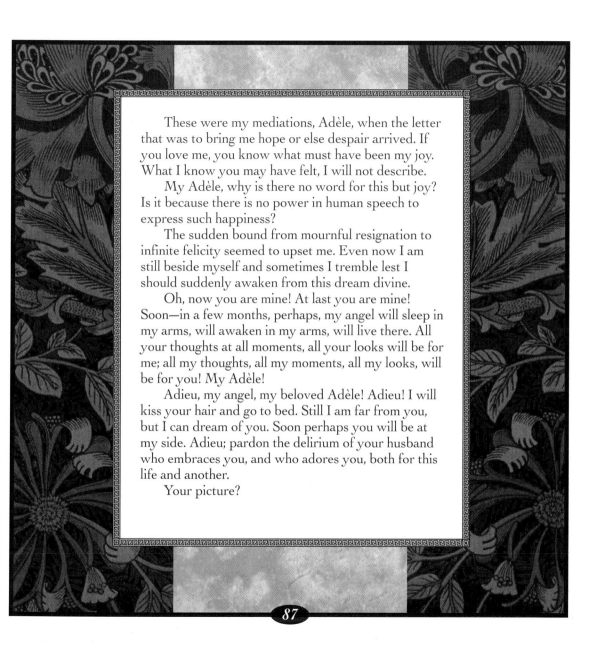

These were my mediations, Adèle, when the letter that was to bring me hope or else despair arrived. If you love me, you know what must have been my joy. What I know you may have felt, I will not describe.

My Adèle, why is there no word for this but joy? Is it because there is no power in human speech to express such happiness?

The sudden bound from mournful resignation to infinite felicity seemed to upset me. Even now I am still beside myself and sometimes I tremble lest I should suddenly awaken from this dream divine.

Oh, now you are mine! At last you are mine! Soon—in a few months, perhaps, my angel will sleep in my arms, will awaken in my arms, will live there. All your thoughts at all moments, all your looks will be for me; all my thoughts, all my moments, all my looks, will be for you! My Adèle!

Adieu, my angel, my beloved Adèle! Adieu! I will kiss your hair and go to bed. Still I am far from you, but I can dream of you. Soon perhaps you will be at my side. Adieu; pardon the delirium of your husband who embraces you, and who adores you, both for this life and another.

Your picture?

First Love

I ne'er was struck before that hour
With love so sudden and so sweet,
Her face it bloomed like a sweet flower
And stole my heart away complete.
My face turned pale as deadly pale.
My legs refused to walk away.
And when she looked, what could I ail?
My life and all seemed turned to clay.

And then my blood rushed to my face
And took my eyesight quite away,
The trees and bushes round the place
Seemed midnight at noonday.
I could not see a single thing,
Words from my eyes did start—
They spoke as chords do from the string,
And blood burnt round my heart.

Are flowers the winter's choice?
Is love's bed always snow?
She seemed to hear my silent voice,
Not love's appeals to know.
I never saw so sweet a face
As that I stood before.
My heart has left its dwelling-place
And can return no more.

—John Clare

Franz Kafka
to
Felice Bauer

Franz Kafka and Felice Bauer

*A*lthough often associated with the dark and brooding qualities of his writings, Franz Kafka (1883-1924), author of such significant novels as *The Trial* and *The Metamorphosis*, possessed passions that ran deeply within him. His love for Felice Bauer, career woman and humanitarian, was not meant to last but lives on in his letters to her.

Kafka met Felice in the home of a mutual friend. They were twice engaged and twice they parted, and ultimately, their engagement was called off. The reasons for this are unknown but it is possible that Kafka's feelings of anxiety and depression as a result of his persistent battle with tuberculosis may have been one factor. Arriving sometimes twice a day, Kafka's letters to Felice have become widely recognized and it is through them that the world gets a glimpse into a different side of this legendary author.

November 11, 1912

Fräulein Felice!

Write to me only once a week, so that your letter arrives on Sunday—for I cannot endure your daily letters, I am incapable of enduring them. For instance, I answer one of your letters, then lie in bed in apparent calm, but my heart beats through my entire body and is conscious only of you. I belong to you; there is not other way of expressing it, and that is not strong enough. But for this very reason I don't want to know what you are wearing; it confuses me so much that I cannot deal with life; and that's why I don't want to know that you are fond of me. If I did, how could I, fool that I am, go on sitting in my office, or here at home, instead of leaping onto a train with my eyes shut and opening them only when I am with you?

June 19, 1913

I want to get married and am so weak that as a
result of a little word on a postcard my knees begin to
shake. Shall I get a letter tomorrow from which I can
conclude that you have carefully considered everything point by point, have fully digested it, and yet say
Yes; in other words that you have not denied everything (that would be unfortunate for, mark my words!
it is undeniable) but invalidated it and surmounted it,
or by virtue of some close reasoning at least are con-
vinced that you are capable of surmounting it?

A life without love is like
a year without summer.
—Swedish Proverb

Let Me Not to the Marriage of True Minds

Let me not to the marriage of true minds
Admit impediments. Love is not love
Which alters when it alteration finds,
Or bends with the remover to remove:
O no; it is an ever-fixed mark,
That looks on tempests, and is never shaken;
It is the star to every wandering bark,
Whose worth's unknown, although his height be
taken,
Love's not Time's fool, though rosy lips and cheeks
Within his bending sickle's compass come;
Love alters not with his brief hours and weeks,
But bears it out even to the edge of doom.
If this be error, and upon me prov'd,
I never writ, nor no man ever lov'd.

—William Shakespeare

To order additional copies of this book, write:

PENBROOKE PUBLISHING, INC.
P.O. Box 700566
Tulsa, OK 74170